CONTENTS

Pedigree

Published by Pedigree Books Limited
Beech Hill House, Walnut Gardens, Exeter, Devon, EX4 4DH
email: books@pedigreegroup.co.uk Published 2006

£7.99

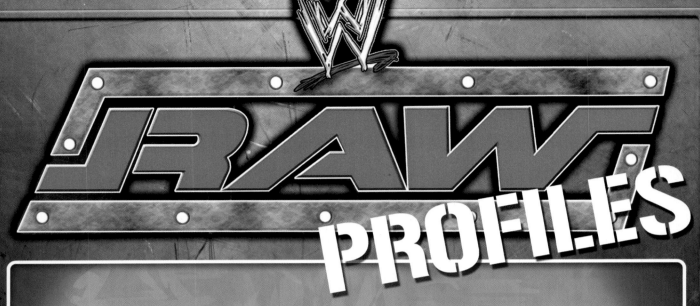

RAW PROFILES

BIG SHOW®

HEIGHT: 7 foot
WEIGHT: 500 pounds
FROM: Tampa, Florida
FINISHING MOVE: ChokeSlam
CAREER HIGHLIGHTS: WWE Champion, WCW Champion, US Champion, Tag Team Champion, ECW Champion

The massive monster has been a force to be reckoned with. One of the largest athletes in the world, the Big Show went into *WrestleMania 22* with his tag team partner Kane to defend the World Tag Team Championship against Carlito & Chris Masters.

KANE

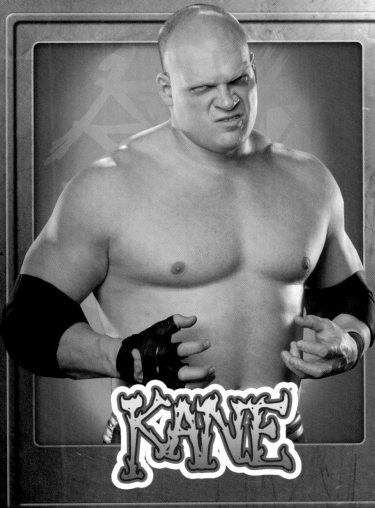

HEIGHT: 7-foot
WEIGHT: 326 pounds
FROM: Unknown
FINISHING MOVE: Chokeslam
CAREER HIGHLIGHTS: WWE Champion, Intercontinental Champion, Tag Team Champion

With the Big Show as his partner, Kane held the World Tag Team Championship for a good portion of 2005 into 2006 and *WrestleMania 22*. "The Big Red Monster" first conquered the world of sports-entertainment, defeating the top superstars in WWE. Kane then set his sights on Hollywood, starring in the horror movie *See No Evil*.

RIC FLAIR

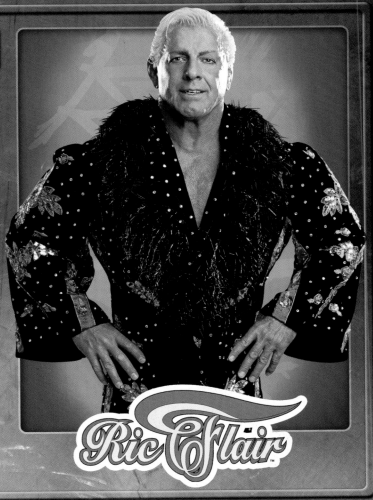

HEIGHT: 6-foot-1
WEIGHT: 243 pounds
FROM: Charlotte, North Carolina
FINISHING MOVE: Figure Four Leglock
CAREER HIGHLIGHTS: WWE Champion, WCW Champion, Intercontinental Champion, United States Champion, Tag Team Champion, *Royal Rumble* Winner

For over 30 years, "The Nature Boy" has proclaimed "To be the man, you've got to beat the man!" And for 30 years, no one has been able to stop him! Holding a World Championship on 16 separate occasions, Ric has proven himself to be a legend. Wooo!

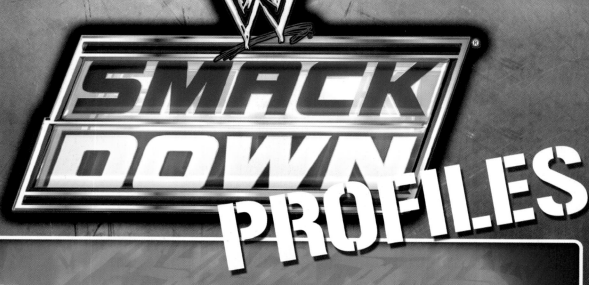

SMACK DOWN PROFILES

CHRIS BENOIT®

HEIGHT: 5-foot-11
WEIGHT: 220 pounds
FROM: Atlanta, Georgia (Originally from Edmonton, Alberta, Canada)
FINISHING MOVE: Crippler Crossface
CAREER HIGHLIGHTS: WWE Champion, WCW Champion, Intercontinental Champion, United States Champion, Tag Team Champion, WCW Television Champion, *Royal Rumble* Winner

He has wrestled all over the world, capturing nearly every major championship in sports-entertainment. He was once a member of the legendary Four Horsemen, and defeated Triple H and Shawn Michaels for the World Heavyweight Championship at *WrestleMania XX*. At *WrestleMania 22* he tangled with JBL, showcasing again why he's called "The Rabid Wolverine."

CHRIS BENOIT

REY MYSTERIO®

HEIGHT: 5-foot-6
WEIGHT: 165 pounds
FROM: San Diego, California
FINISHING MOVE: 619
CAREER HIGHLIGHTS: World Heavyweight Champion, Cruiserweight Champion, WWE Tag Team Champion, WCW Tag Team Champion, *Royal Rumble* Winner

They say it's not the size of the dog in the fight that matters, but the size of the fight in the dog. Rey Mysterio proves that's true every time he enters the ring. He's small, but has accomplished more than many men larger than he. At *WrestleMania 22*, he fought Randy Orton and Kurt Angle and won the World Heavyweight Championship, dedicating the match to his best friend (and 2006 Hall of Fame inductee) the late Eddie Guerrero.

BATISTA™

HEIGHT: 6-foot-5
WEIGHT: 317 pounds
FROM: Washington D.C.
FINISHING MOVE: Batista Bomb
CAREER HIGHLIGHTS: World Heavyweight Champion, World Tag Team Champion, *Royal Rumble* Winner, WWE Tag Team Champion

He's called "The Animal", and for good reason! With his devastating Batista Bomb, Batista has defeated some of the best in sports-entertainment history. A former member of Evolution, The Animal forfeited his World Heavyweight Championship because of an injury in late 2005, but returned in early 2006 on a mission to recapture the gold.

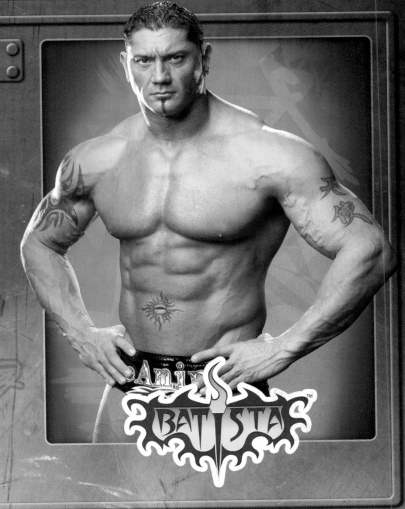

GOLDUST™

HEIGHT: 6-foot-6
WEIGHT: 260 pounds
FROM: Hollywood, California
FINISHING MOVE: Curtain Call
CAREER HIGHLIGHTS: Intercontinental Champion, World Tag Team Champion

The Bizarre One, Goldust, has taunted WWE Superstars with his mind games since his debut in 1995. Don't let his strange appearance fool you; he is an extremely talented wrestler. He has held the Intercontinental and World Tag Team championships on many occasions, and can defeat seemingly any WWE Superstar.

TREVOR MURDOCH™

HEIGHT: 6-foot-4
WEIGHT: 241 pounds
FROM: Waxahachie, Texas
FINISHING MOVE: Top Rope Bulldog
CAREER HIGHLIGHTS: World Tag Team Champion

Tough as nails, this Texas brawler was trained by WWE Hall of Famer Harley Race. Dressed in blue jeans and cutoff shirts, Murdock is a mean, violent man in the ring. He is determined to make his mark on the WWE, even applying to be the general manager of *Raw*!

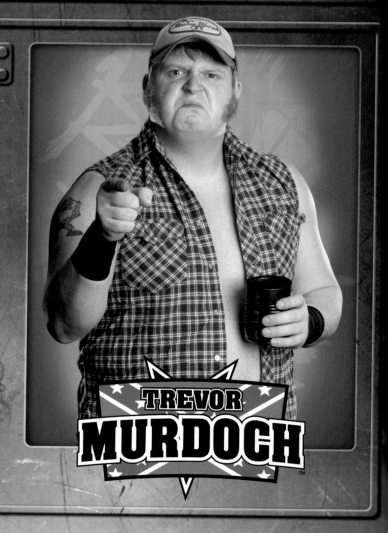

TREVOR MURDOCH™

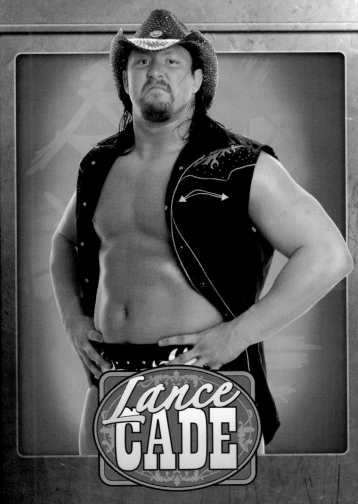

LANCE CADE

HEIGHT: 6-foot-5
WEIGHT: 261 pounds
FROM: Nashville, Tennessee
FINISHING MOVE: Lariat Clothesline
CAREER HIGHLIGHTS: World Tag Team Champion

He may look like a "good ol' boy," but Lance Cade is one mean Southerner. Like his tag team partner, Trevor Murdock, Cade is a tough brawler in the ring. Though he wears high-dollar clothes to the ring, Cade has proven over the years that he can out fight just about anyone, even once winning the World Tag Team Championship.

HULK HOGAN

HEIGHT: 6-foot-7
FROM: Venice Beach, California
FINISHING MOVE: Legdrop
CAREER HIGHLIGHTS: WWE Champion, WCW Champion, World Tag Team Champion, WWE Tag Team Champion, *Royal Rumble* Winner, WWE Hall of Fame (Inducted in 2005)

In the worlds of sports and entertainment, few have accomplished as much as the Immortal Hulk Hogan. Since *Hulkamania* began running wild in the 1980s, Hogan has won world championships, appeared in movies, and faced the biggest names in wrestling history.

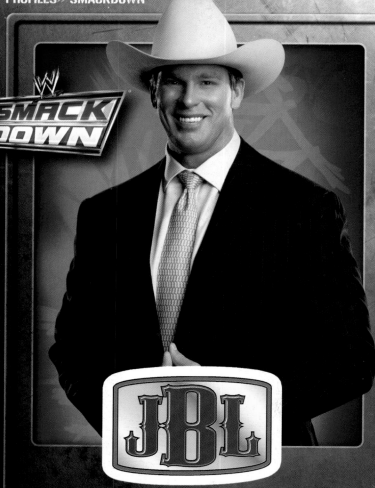

JBL™

HEIGHT: 6-foot-6
WEIGHT: 290 pounds
FROM: New York City
FINISHING MOVE: Clothesline from Hell
CAREER HIGHLIGHTS: WWE Champion, World Tag Team Champion

Radio Talk show Host, Financial Advisor, and self-proclaimed "Wrestling God," JBL wears many hats outside the squared circle. But in the ring, he's a powerful force to be reckoned with – something Chris Benoit found out at WrestleMania 22 when the two wrestled for the United States Championship.

THE GREAT KHALI™

HEIGHT: 7-foot-3
WEIGHT: 420 pounds
FROM: India

After the Undertaker buried Mark Henry at a *WrestleMania 22* casket match, Henry's manager went to India to find a monster big enough to destroy Undertaker. There he discovered The Great Khali. One of the biggest men to ever enter WWE, he has his sights set on the "Deadman"!

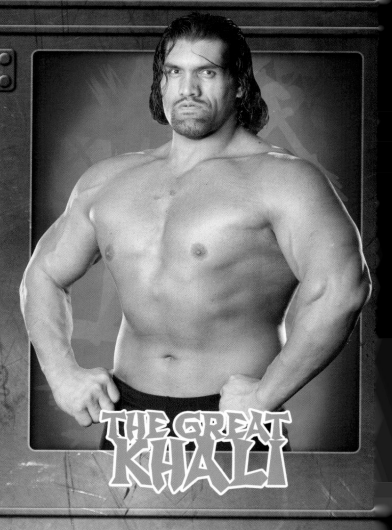

TAZZ™

HEIGHT: 5-foot-9
WEIGHT: 252 pounds
FROM: Red Hook Section of Brooklyn, New York
FINISHING MOVE: Tazzmission
CAREER HIGHLIGHTS: ECW Champion, World Tag Team Champion, ECW Tag Team Champion, ECW Television Champion

Known as the "Human Suplex Machine", Tazz was a force to be reckoned with the late 1990s and early 2000s. Coming to WWE from ECW, where he was a vicious monster in the ring, he discovered his love of announcing. He is now the color commentator for ECW.

TATANKA™

HEIGHT: 6-Foot-2
WEIGHT: 258 Pounds
FROM: Pembroke, North Carolina
FINISHING MOVE: The Trail's End
CAREER HIGHLIGHTS: Undefeated in WWE for nearly two years in 1991-1993

After several years the mighty Native American warrior Tatanka returned to WWE with a vengeance. Though he did not recapture his unprecedented undefeated streak from 1991-1993, he has proven that he is not out of step, and is again a powerful force in WWE.

TATANKA

Divas Profiles

Trish Stratus®

From: Toronto, Ontario, Canada

Finishing Move: Stratusfaction, Chick Kick

Career Highlights: WWE Women's Champion

A hard-working, talented WWE Diva, Trish began as a manager for tag teams, but soon found herself inside the ring. She has defeated the top women in WWE. Her feud with Mickie James culminated in a match for the Women's Championship at *WrestleMania 22*. Though she lost the title to Mickie, you can bet Trish will do whatever she has to, to get it back soon!

Maria™

From: Ottawa, Illinois

Finishing Move: 2004 *Raw* Diva Search Contestant; *Raw* Backstage Interviewer

She may be one of the prettiest WWE Divas, but Maria has shown herself to be a bit oblivious when it comes to interviewing the WWE Superstars. In spite of this, she is popular among fans – especially with her WWE Unlimited segment, "Kiss Cam" where she focuses the camera on *Raw* audience members, inviting couples to kiss!

Candice Michelle™

From: Milwaukee, Wisconsin

She's been called too hot for TV, appeared in commercials shown during the Super Bowl, and made her presence felt on *Raw*. Candice may not have held the Women's Championship, but she is one of the most popular Divas in WWE history. She recently turned on her friend Torrie Wilson, and with the help of fellow Diva, Victoria, has promised to make Torrie's life miserable, even fighting her at *WrestleMania 22*.

KANE & BIG SHOW
VS
CARLITO & MASTERS

HERE WE ARE AT WRESTLEMANIA 22, WHERE THE WORLD TAG TEAM CHAMPIONSHIP IS GOING TO BE DEFENDED!

HERE'S ONE-HALF OF THE CHALLENGERS, "THE MASTERPIECE" CHRIS MASTERS!

LOOK AT THE MUSCLES ON MASTERS!

HE AND HIS TAG TEAM PARTNER, CARLITO, COULD POSE A THREAT TO THE CHAMPIONS!

BIG SHOW WITH THE BIG SLAM ON MASTERS!

MASTERS TAGGED IN CARLITO, WHO LOOKS A LITTLE INTIMIDATED BY BIG SHOW.

AS HE SHOULD! BIG SHOW LIFTS CARLITO UP BY ONE ARM.

AND SETS HIM DOWN ON THE ROPE. THAT'S GOT TO HURT!

CARLITO IS IN TROUBLE.

MASTERS TRIED TO SAVE CARLITO, BUT ONLY FOUND HIMSELF IN BIGGER TROUBLE!

CARLITO GETS LIFTED FOR A BIG SLAM, TOO!

WATCH OUT MASTERS! BIG SHOW IS THROWING YOUR PARTNER AT YOU!

KANE FLIES TO THE OUTSIDE.

THIS GIVES CARLITO A CHANCE TO GO AFTER BIG SHOW.

KANE GETS HIT, TOO.

MASTERS GETS KANE IN THE UNBREAKABLE MASTERLOCK! NO ONE CAN GET OUT OF THIS!

KANE GOT FREE. CARLITO IS IN DANGER, CAN MASTERS MAKE THE SAVE?

CARLITO TURNS IT AROUND, AND ATTACKS KANE WITH A BACKBREAKER.

BUT KANE REBOUNDS QUICKLY, AND POUNDS CARLITO IN THE CORNER.

KANE WITH A HUGE CHOKESLAM ON CARLITO. THIS HAS GOT TO BE THE END!

HE'S GOING TO LAND HARD.

YOUR WINNERS, AND STILL WORLD TAG TEAM CHAMPIONS!

KANE & BIG SHOW!

WELL, WHADDAYA KNOW?
QUIZ

Think you know the *Raw* Superstars? Take this quiz and see if you know enough to call yourself Champion! Answers are below.

1

Goldust is the son of which WWE Legend?
A) Billy Graham
B) Dusty Rhodes
C) Hulk Hogan

2

Ric Flair was NOT a member of which team?
A) The Fabulous Freebirds
B) Four Horsemen
C) Evolution

3

What championship did Rob Van Dam hold for 22 months?
A) ECW Television Championship
B) WWE Intercontinental Championship
C) U.S. Championship

4

Which Diva has never won the WWE Women's Championship?
A) Trish Stratus
B) Victoria
C) Candice Michelle

5

How many WWE Superstars are members of the Spirit Squad?
A) Four
B) Five
C) Six

6

Who is Lita's boyfriend?
A) Snitsky
B) Kane
C) Edge

RAW

7

What is the name of John Cena's Rap Album?
A) *"The Champ is Here"*
B) *"Chain Gang Nation"*
C) *"You Can't See Me"*

8

Where did Shelton Benjamin attend university?
A) Colorado State University
B) University of Minnesota
C) Duke University

9

In what company did announcer Jerry Lawler make his name?
A) ECW
B) USWA
C) WCW

10

What is the name of Kane's movie debut?
A) *See No Evil*
B) *Hear No Evil*
C) *Speak No Evil*

11

Who was Shawn Michaels's tag team partner in "The Rockers?"
A) Triple H
B) Marty Jannetty
C) Diesel

So, how'd you do?
10-11: You are the Champion!
7-9: You are the number one contender!
4-6: Keep working out.
2-3: You got pinned.
0-1: Sorry, better keep watching.

CHRIS BENOIT vs JBL

CAN YOU BELIEVE THIS! JBL IS DRIVING HIS LIMO INTO THE ARENA!

HE'S COMPETING FOR THE UNITED STATES CHAMPIONSHIP AGAINST CHRIS BENOIT, AND IS COMING TO THE RING IN A CAR!

JBL IS CERTAINLY CONFIDENT!

HE WANTS TO PROVE THAT HE IS THE GREATEST TECHNICAL WRESTLER OF ALL TIME.

BUT THE UNITED STATES CHAMPION, CHRIS BENOIT, STANDS IN HIS WAY.

THIS SHOULD BE A GREAT CONTEST!

THESE TWO SUPERSTARS ARE INTENSE, AND READY FOR A GREAT MATCH.

IT'S FOR THE UNITED STATES CHAMPIONSHIP - A TITLE BOTH MEN WANT.

THE REFEREE IS GETTING THEM READY.

JBL'S TRASH TALK WON'T PHASE "THE CRIPPLER" CHRIS BENOIT.

AND THEY'RE OFF! LOCKING UP WITH A COLLAR/ELBOW TIE-UP!

BENOIT LANDS A HUGE HIT!

HE'S JUST POUNDING AWAY ON JBL IN THE CORNER!

BUT JBL GETS OUT, AND LANDS SOME POWERFUL HITS OF HIS OWN.

JBL IS TAKING CONTROL OF THE MATCH WITH A HEADLOCK.

BENOIT IS IN A HEAP OF TROUBLE. HE COULD LOSE THE MATCH AND THE TITLE VERY QUICKLY HERE.

THERE CAN'T BE MUCH LEFT IN BENOIT.

WAIT A MINUTE! BENOIT IS FIGHTING HIS WAY OUT OF THE HOLD!

HE'S REVERSING IT INTO A HOLD OF HIS OWN.

HE'S TRYING FOR THE CRIPPLER CROSSFACE. WILL HE LOCK IT IN?

HE DOES! HE'S BEATEN SOME OF THE BEST IN THE BUSINESS WITH THIS HOLD. WILL HE BEAT JBL, TOO?

JBL BREAKS FREE FROM BENOIT'S GRIP, AND LANDS A MIGHTY KICK.

BUT BENOIT BOUNCES BACK, AND GOES FOR THE SHARPSHOOTER.

JBL ESCAPES YET ANOTHER HOLD, AND IS FIRING BACK WITH A SERIES OF RIGHT HANDS.

BENOIT RETURNS FIRE WITH A BIG HEADBUTT.

THIS IS AN AMAZING BACK-AND-FORTH CONTEST, AS JBL RETAKES CONTROL.

BUT IT HAS NO EFFECT, AND JBL GOES FOR A SERIES OF SUPLEXES.

AND NOW BENOIT REVERSES FORTUNES, AND GOES FOR HIS PATENTED FLYING HEADBUTT!

THE SUPLEXES WORKED, AND JBL HAS DEFEATED CHRIS BENOIT TO WIN THE UNITED STATES CHAMPIONSHIP.

JBL AND HIS ADVISER JILLIAN CELEBRATE THEIR VICTORY.

JBL IS THE UNITED STATES CHAMPION!

HALL OF FAME
WORD SEARCH

Every year, during *WrestleMania* weekend, the WWE welcomes past Superstars into the "Hall of Fame". See if you can find the term "Hall of Fame" and the names of the Superstars inducted this year, as well as the Superstars who inducted them. They read forward, backward, up, down and diagonal.

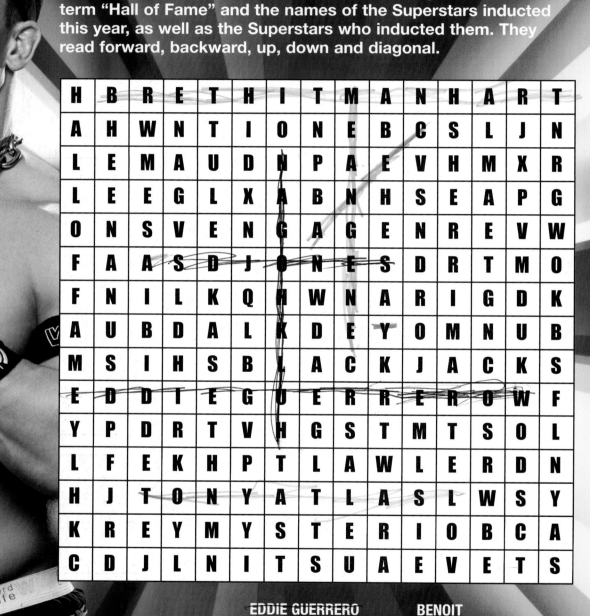

H	B	R	E	T	H	I	T	M	A	N	H	A	R	T
A	H	W	N	T	I	O	N	E	B	C	S	L	J	N
L	E	M	A	U	D	N	P	A	E	V	H	M	X	R
L	E	E	G	L	X	A	B	N	H	S	E	A	P	G
O	N	S	V	E	N	G	A	G	E	N	R	E	V	W
F	A	A	S	D	J	O	N	E	S	D	R	T	M	O
F	N	I	L	K	Q	H	W	N	A	R	I	G	D	K
A	U	B	D	A	L	K	D	E	Y	O	M	N	U	B
M	S	I	H	S	B	L	A	C	K	J	A	C	K	S
E	E	D	D	I	E	G	U	E	R	R	E	R	O	W	F
Y	P	D	R	T	V	H	G	S	T	M	T	S	O	L
L	F	E	K	H	P	T	L	A	W	L	E	R	D	N
H	J	T	O	N	Y	A	T	L	A	S	L	W	S	Y
K	R	E	Y	M	Y	S	T	E	R	I	O	B	C	A
C	D	J	L	N	I	T	S	U	A	E	V	E	T	S

EDDIE GUERRERO BENOIT
S.D. JONES BRET "HIT MAN" HART
HULK HOGAN REY MYSTERIO
CENA TED DIBIASE
MEAN GENE LAWLER
TONY ATLAS CHAVO
VERNE GAGNE HEENAN
STEVE AUSTIN BLACKJACKS
SHERRI MARTEL PERRY

WINNERS AND LOSERS
CROSSWORD

There were a lots of winners and, of course, some losers at *WrestleMania 22*. See if you can identify which WWE Superstars won their match at *WrestleMania*, and which lost. Fill in the crossword puzzle with each Superstar's name.

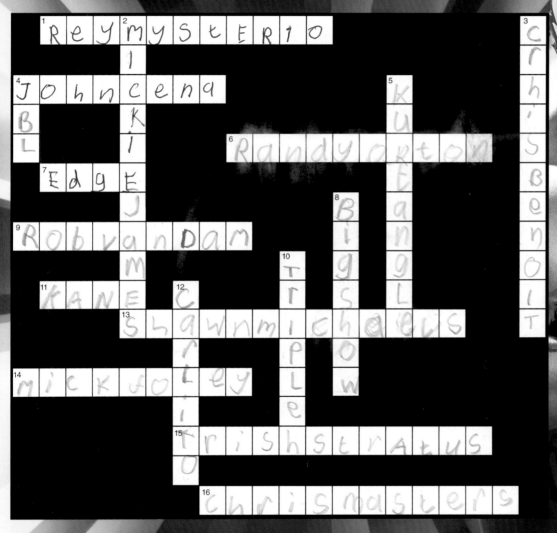

Crossword answers:
1. Rey Mysterio
4. John Cena
6. Randy Orton
7. Edge
9. Rob Van Dam
11. Kane
13. Shawn Michaels
14. Mick Foley
15. Trish Stratus
16. Chris Masters

Down:
2. Mickie James
3. Chris Benoit
5. Kurt Angle
8. Big Show
10. Triple H
12. Carlito

ACROSS
1. World Heavyweight Championship (Won)
4. WWE Championship (Won)
6. World Heavyweight Championship (Lost)
7. Hardcore Winner (Won)
9. Money In The Bank (Won)
11. World Tag Team Championship (Won)
13. No Holds Barred (Won)
14. Hardcore Match (Lost)
15. Women's Championship (Lost)
16. World Tag Team Championship (Lost)

DOWN
2. Women's Championship (Won)
3. United States Championship (Lost)
4. United States Championship (Won)
5. World Heavyweight Championship (Lost)
8. World Tag Team Championship (Won)
10. WWE Championship (Lost)
12. World Tag Team Championship (Lost)

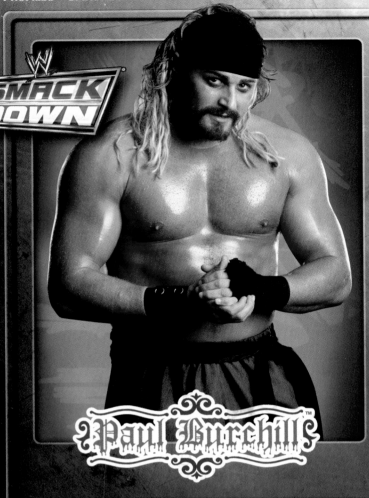

Paul Burchill

PAUL BURCHILL™

HEIGHT: 6-foot-4
WEIGHT: 268 pounds
FROM: St. Thomas in the Virgin Islands
FINISHING MOVE: Backflip Uranage Slam

A pirate's life is the one chosen for SmackDown! Superstar Paul Burchill. With painful submission holds and the stunning Backflip Uranage Slam in his arsenal, Paul Burchill has shown that he is a tough opponent for anyone he faces.

MATT HARDY™

HEIGHT: 6-foot-2
WEIGHT: 225 pounds
FROM: Cameron, North Carolina
FINISHING MOVE: Twist of Fate
CAREER HIGHLIGHTS: European Champion, World Tag Team Champion, Cruiserweight Champion, WCW Tag Team Champion

Whenever fans hear the scream "Oh yeeeaaahhh!" they know Matt Hardy is on his way. Hardy has thrilled WWE fans for nearly a decade with his high impact, high flying style and intense ring persona.

Matt Hardy

GREGORY HELMS

HEIGHT: 6-foot
WEIGHT: 215 pounds
FROM: Smithfield, North Carolina
FINISHING MOVE: Shining Wizard
CAREER HIGHLIGHTS: Cruiserweight Champion, World Tag Team Champion

By the invitation from *SmackDown* general manager Theodore Long, Helms entered a Battle Royale for the Cruiserweight Championship. Having left behind his comic book-like character, The Hurricane, Helms displayed a new violent intensity, winning the match and the title.

BOOGEYMAN

FROM: The Bottomless Pit

He lives off of others' fear and paranoia. From you worst nightmares, the worm-munching monster has haunted *SmackDown*'s superstars like Booker T and JBL. He has attacked Divas such as Sharmell and Jillian Hall, too. No one knows when to expect him, and that is the scariest part of all.

THE BOOGEYMAN

CHARLIE HAAS™

HEIGHT: 6-foot-2
WEIGHT: 242 pounds
FROM: Edmond, Oklahoma
FINISHING MOVE: Folding neck/back submission
CAREER HIGHLIGHTS: WWE Tag Team Champion

Charlie Haas is a technical wizard in the ring. His former associations with Kurt Angle and Shelton Benjamin allowed him many opportunities to display his phenomenal technical abilities. Returning to WWE shortly after *WrestleMania 22*, Haas is back in the hunt for the top spots in the company, again using his amazing abilities.

SHELTON BENJAMIN™

HEIGHT: 6-foot-2
WEIGHT: 245 pounds
FROM: Orangeburg, South Carolina
FINISHING MOVE: T-Bone Suplex
CAREER HIGHLIGHTS: Intercontinental Champion, WWE Tag Team Championship

Shelton's music begins with the phrase "There's no stopping me now!" A former collegiate champion, Shelton burst onto the WWE scene as a member of Team Angle. Winning the Intercontinental and Tag Team Championships showed that he was rising to the top.

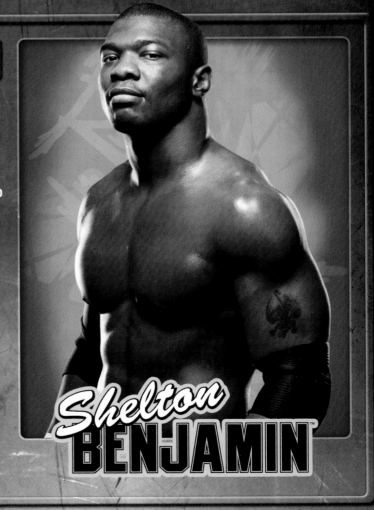

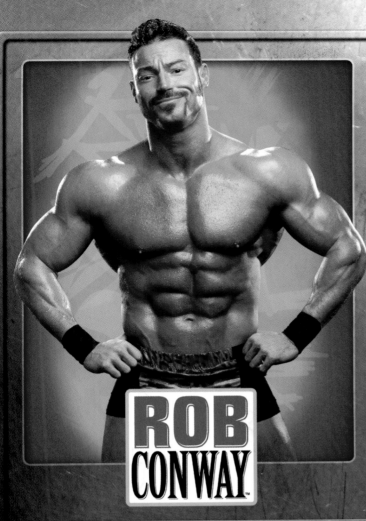

ROB CONWAY™

HEIGHT: 6-foot-2
WEIGHT: 230 pounds
FROM: Atlantic City, New Jersey
FINISHING MOVE: Ego Trip
CAREER HIGHLIGHTS: World Tag Team Champion

A former World Tag Team Champion, Conway has moved on to the singles ranks. Trying to make a name for himself by attacking WWE legends like Koko B. Ware, Jimmy Snuka, and Grag Valentine, Conway is a rising star on Raw. Where his talents and ego take him remains to be seen, but one thing's for sure: he thinks it will be to the top!

CHRIS MASTERS™

HEIGHT: 6-foot-4
WEIGHT: 275 pounds
FROM: Los Angeles, California
FINISHING MOVE: Masterlock

With an amazing chiseled body, and an unbreakable finishing hold (the Masterlock), Chis Masters is well on his way to dominance in WWE. Whether facing off against his former friend and tag team partner Carlito, or stomping contestants in the Masterlock Challenge, Chris Masters knows he's the best wrestler on *Raw*, and will prove it to anyone who dares question him.

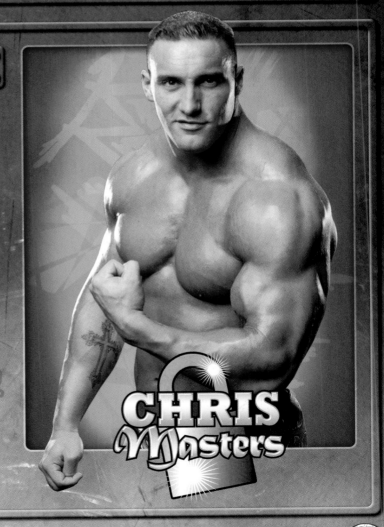

SMACK DOWN

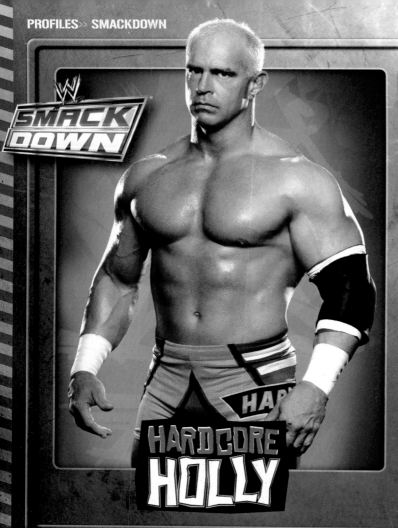

HARDCORE HOLLY™

HEIGHT: 6 foot
WEIGHT: 235 pounds
FROM: Mobile, Alabama
FINISHING MOVE: Alabama Slam
CAREER HIGHLIGHTS: World Tag Team Champion

The former World Tag Team Championship is mean. His intensity in the ring, and his dedication to winning matches have allowed him to prove his dominance over many an opponent. Hardcore Holly is a believer in hard work, and dedication and has no patience for those who don't want to work hard.

HARDCORE HOLLY

BRIAN KENDRICK™

HEIGHT: 5-foot-8
WEIGHT: 175 pounds
FROM: Olympia, Washington
FINISHING MOVE: Sliced Bread #2; Dr. Smoothe's Secret Recipe

This high-flying cruiserweight recently returned to WWE after a brief hiatus to hone his skills. Trained in Japanese dojos, and by WWE Legend Shawn Michaels, Kendrick has overcome the odds and shown that size is not a factor in being successful in WWE rings.

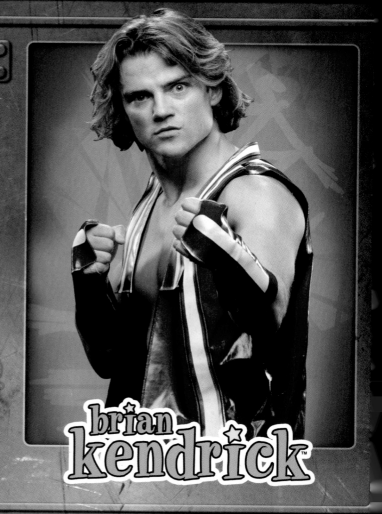

brian kendrick™

KID KASH™

HEIGHT: 5-foot-10
WEIGHT: 199 pounds
FROM: Johnson City, Tennessee
FINISHING MOVE: Dead Level
CAREER HIGHLIGHTS: Cruiserweight Champion, ECW Television Champion

With an intense passion for action, Kid Kash has used his high-flying techniques to make a name for himself in ECW, winning it's Television Championship. His tenure in WWE has been just as successful, as he has defeated nearly everyone in the Cruiserweight division, and held that title as well.

JAIME NOBLE™

HEIGHT: 5-foot-9
WEIGHT: 202 pounds
FROM: Hanover, West Virginia
FINISHING MOVE: Modified Dragon Sleeper
CAREER HIGHLIGHTS: Cruiserweight Championship

A hardened "country boy," Noble has the honor of being one of WWE's longest-reining Cruiserweight Champions. His memorable run as champ in 2002 proved him to be a powerful force in the Cruiserweight division. His recent return to WWE reminded fans and WWE Superstars why he held the title for so long – a record he wants to break himself.

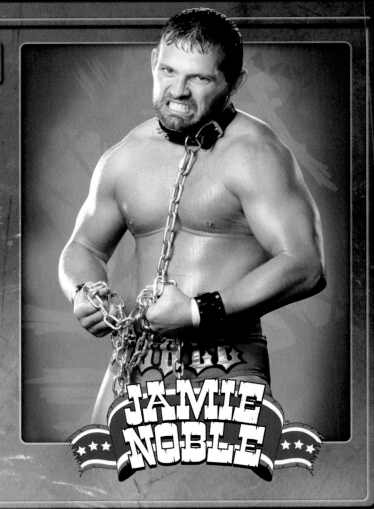

JAMIE NOBLE

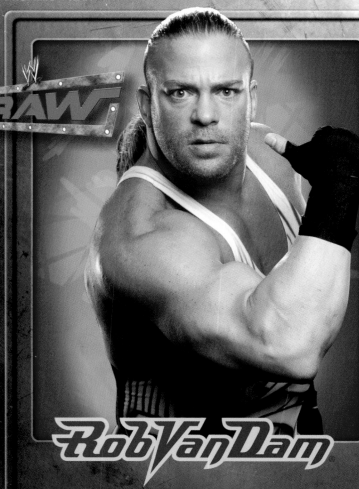

ROB VAN DAM

HEIGHT: 6-foot
WEIGHT: 235 pounds
FROM: Battle Creek, Michigan
FINISHING MOVE: 5-Star Frog Splash, Van Daminator, Van Terminator
CAREER HIGHLIGHTS: ECW World Champion, WWE Champion, Intercontinental Champion, World Tag Team Champion, WWE Tag Team Champion, ECW Television Champion, ECW Tag Team Champion, Money in the Bank Winner

Since returning to WWE at the 2006 *Royal Rumble*, RVD has dominated Raw. By winning the Money in the Bank ladder match at *WrestleMania 22*, Mr. Monday Night won the WWE Championship at One Night Stand and was awarded the ECW World Championship two nights later.

JOEY STYLES™

FROM: Stamford, Connecticut
CAREER HIGHLIGHTS: Lead Announcer for ECW

No matter how good a wrestling match is, a good announcer makes it better, and Joey Styles is one of the best. Also a talented writer and reporter, Styles adds a vast depth of knowledge to the ECW announcing team.

JOHN CENA®

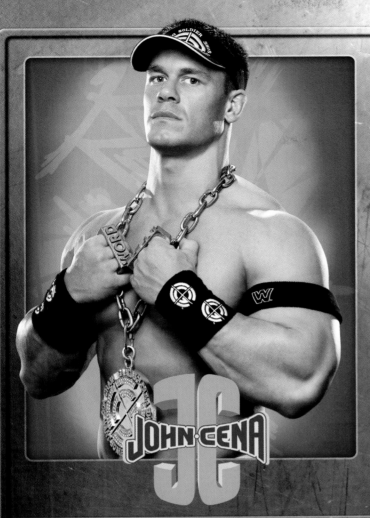

HEIGHT: 6-foot-1
WEIGHT: 240 pounds
FROM: West Newbury, Massachusetts
FINISHING MOVE: FU, STFU, Five Knuckle Shuffle
CAREER HIGHLIGHTS: WWE Champion, United States Champion

He shocked the world by defeating Triple H at *WrestleMania 22.* "The Champ" John Cena has overcome threats from Edge, Triple H, and others retaining his WWE Championship. He will also make his feature film debut in *The Marine.*

EDGE®

HEIGHT: 6-foot-5
WEIGHT: 240 pounds
FROM: Toronto, Ontario, Canada
FINISHING MOVE: Spear
CAREER HIGHLIGHTS: WWE Champion, World Tag Team Champion, WWE Tag Team Champion, Intercontinental Champion, United States Champion

"The Rated-R Superstar" has proven to be a formidable opponent and a threat to anyone who possesses a WWE Championship. He faced "The Hardcore Legend" Mick Foley at *WrestleMania 22,* beating Mick at his own game. He promised that it will only be a matter of time before he regains the WWE Championship, a vow he fulfilled two months later.

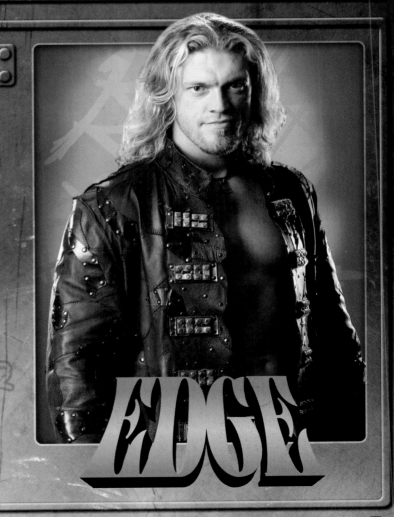

Mickie James ™

Height: **5-Foot-4**

From: **Richmond, Virginia**

Finishing Move: **Mick Kick**

Career Highlights: **WWE Women's Champion**

Debuting as Trish Stratus' biggest fan, Mickie James turned from fan to nemesis, defeating her idol for the Women's Championship at *WrestleMania 22*. Often called "psycho," Mickie has made an effort to "become" Trish by dressing like her, and doing her same wrestling moves.

Lita ®

Height: **5-foot-6**

From: **Sanford, North Carolina**

Finishing Move: **Moonsault, DDT**

Career Highlights: **WWE Women's Champion**

She's beautiful but dangerous. Lita is a talented ring technician, but she is also a heartbreaker. She's known for her torrid relationships with Matt Hardy, Kane, and now Edge. Always by her man's side (whomever that man is), Lita is an asset, leading them to championships, but eventually destroying them, too. Watch out for this wily Diva!

Sharmell ™

From: Houston, Texas

Career Highlights: 1991 Miss Black America

Not every Diva can claim the title of being a true beauty queen, but Sharmell can! But don't let her looks fool you – she is sneaky, having helped her husband, Booker T, capture titles. After overcoming attacks from the Boogeyman prior to *WrestleMania 22*, Sharmell has proven that she can handle anything the WWE may have in store!

Torrie Wilson ®

Height: 5-foot-7

From: Boise, Idaho

Finishing Move: Springboard Elbow

She's made the other Divas jealous just by being stunningly beautiful. But that's not all this Diva has done! She has managed some of the top WWE Superstars, and even hosted special programming on WWE.com. With her trusty puppy Chloe by her side, Torrie turns heads and attracts attention wherever she goes.

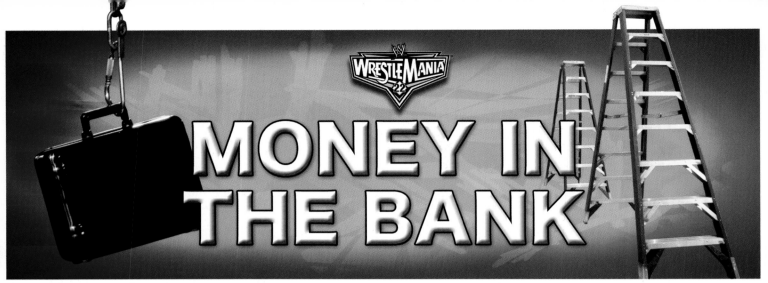

MONEY IN THE BANK

THE RULES ARE SIMPLE. THE FIRST SUPERSTAR TO CLIMB A LADDER AND GET THE BRIEFCASE HANGING ABOVE THE RING WILL WIN THE MATCH, AND GET A WORLD TITLE SHOT WHENEVER HE WANTS IT!

HERE COMES MATT HARDY! HE'S THE FIRST OF SIX WWE SUPERSTARS TO ENTER THIS MATCH.

HERE'S LASHLEY!

HE'S ONE TOUGH SUPERSTAR. HE'S GOT TO BE A FAVOURITE IN THIS MATCH.

ROB VAN DAM ENTERS THE ARENA!

AND THE MATCH BEGINS AS FINLAY AND LASHLEY TAKE TO ONE ANOTHER.

LOOK AT THE POWER LASHLEY HAS AS HE HOISTS RIC FLAIR OVER HIS HEAD.

MATT HARDY ON THE ATTACK.

RVD SLAMS INTO HARDY WITH THE LADDER!

AND NOW SHELTON BENJAMIN WITH AN AMAZING DIVE!

BACK IN THE RING, RIC FLAIR IS NEAR THE BRIEFCASE!

BENJAMIN CRASHES INTO THREE OTHER WWE SUPERSTARS. DID THAT HURT HIM MORE THAN THEM?

MATT HARDY STANDS BETWEEN FLAIR AND THE BRIEFCASE.

FLAIR REACHES AGAIN FOR THE BRIEFCASE, BUT FINLAY FOLLOWED HIM BACK INTO THE RING.

FLAIR DOESN'T GET IT, BUT HE DOES GET TO POUND ON FINLAY IN THE OUTSIDE.

FLAIR IS A 16-TIME WORLD CHAMPION. GETTING THE BRIEFCASE COULD MEAN ONE MORE, AND YOU KNOW HE WANTS IT!

THE ACTION IS FAST AND FURIOUS IN THE RING. SO MANY WWE SUPERSTARS WANT THAT BRIEFCASE.

RVD LANDS A HUGE DROPKICK WITH A CHAIR, SAVING THE BRIEFCASE.

LASHLEY'S GOT TO BE FEELING THAT.

WITH LASHLEY DOWN AFTER THAT KICK FROM RVD, MATT HARDY LOOKS TO WIN THE PRIZE.

WAIT A MINUTE. HARDY'S NOT GOING FOR THE BRIEFCASE. WHAT'S HE DOING?

LOOK AT THAT LEGDROP ON LASHLEY FROM THE TOP OF THE LADDER!

IT'S A LONG WAY DOWN FROM THE TOP OF THE LADDER. HARDY COULD LAND HARD!

LASHLEY IS IN SERIOUS TROUBLE.

RVD GETS THE BRIEFCASE! YOU CAN CALL HIM 'MR. MONEY IN THE BANK!'

FROM HIS TIME IN ECW UNTIL NOW, RVD HAS SEARCHED FOR A WORLD TITLE SHOT. NOW HE GETS IT WHENEVER HE WANTS IT!

HE'S GOING TO TAKE IT TO THE EXTREME!

ROB VAN DAM DEFEATED FIVE OTHER WWE SUPERSTARS IN ONE AMAZING MATCH!

WELL, WHADDAYA KNOW? QUIZ

Think you know the SmackDown Superstars? Take this quiz and see if you know enough to call yourself Champion! Answers are below.

1

What is the Boogeyman's favourite food?
A) Grasshoppers
B) Worms
C) Flies

2

Who was Gregory Helms previously known as?
A) Umanga
B) Goldust
C) The Hurricane

3

Which of the following is NOT one of Kurt Angle's "Three I's?"
A) Intensity
B) Intelligence
C) Icon

4

Who is Booker T's wife?
A) Victoria
B) Sharmell
C) Melina

5

What does "JBL" stand for?
A) John "Bradshaw" Layfield
B) Justin Brady Lee
C) Jerry B. Light

6

Chris Benoit was never a member of which team?
A) Four Horsemen
B) Radicalz
C) D-Generation X

7

Joey Mercury and Johnny Nitro, along with Melina, make up which team?
A) The Hollywood Blondes
B) The Heart Throbs
C) MNM

8

Who managed both Kurt Angle and Mark Henry?
A) Daivari
B) Melina
C) Paul Bearer

9

To whom did Rey Mysterio dedicate his Royal Rumble and *WrestleMania 22* matches?
A) Brian Pillman
B) Eddie Guerrero
C) Owen Hart

10

What major championship did announcer Tazz hold?
A) WCW Championship
B) WWE Championship
C) ECW Championship

11

How many matches has the Undertaker won at WrestleMania?
A) 14
B) 16
C) 18

12

Who has never been a SmackDown General Manager?
A) Shane McMahon
B) Stephanie McMahon
C) Paul Heyman

Answers: 1.B 2.C 3.C 4.B 5.A 6.C 7.C 8.A 9.B 10.C 11.A 12.A

So, how'd you do?
11-12: You are the Champion!
8-10: You are the number one contender!
5-7: Keep working out.
2-4: You got pinned.
0-1: Sorry, better keep watching.

REY MYSTERIO
vs
KURT ANGLE
vs
RANDY ORTON

HE WON THE ROYAL RUMBLE, EARNING HIM A SHOT AT THE WORLD HEAVYWEIGHT CHAMPIONSHIP! AND HERE HE IS! REY MYSTERIO!

POPPING UP THROUGH THE FLOOR! WHAT AN ENTRANCE FOR THE 5-FOOT-6 COMPETITOR!

AND THAT COLOURFUL ATTIRE! MYSTERIO IS READY!

MYSTERIO DEDICATED THIS MATCH TO THE MEMORY OF HIS FRIEND, THE LATE EDDIE GUERRERO.

MYSTERIO, ANGLE, AND ORTON STARE EACH OTHER DOWN! WHO WILL SCORE THE FIRST PIN AND BECOME THE WORLD HEAVYWEIGHT CHAMPION?

RANDY ORTON CATCHES MYSTERIO WITH A BIG KICK!

BUT ANGLES SUPLEXES ORTON FROM BEHIND.

ANGLE LOOKS CONFIDENT!

56

ANGLE'S SUPLEXES CAN DO A LOT OF DAMAGE.

LOOK AT THAT! AN AMAZING THREE-MAN SUPLEX!

MYSTERIO FINALLY STRIKES BACK WITH A BIG KICK ON ANGLE.

BUT ANGLE WILL HAVE NONE OF THAT! HE RETURNS WITH A BIG HIT TO THE FACE!

ORTON SMASHES ANGLE!

WHERE DID MYSTERIO COME FROM?

THOSE KICKS ARE BRUTAL.

A PIN! WILL HE GET HIM?

NO! THE MATCH CONTINUES WITH REY MYSTERIO GOING FOR HIS PATENTED 619.

FIRST A 619 ON ORTON, NOW ONE ON ANGLE!

KURT ANGLE RESPONDS BY LOCKING IN HIS DEVASTATING ANKLE LOCK.

ORTON BREAKS IT UP.

ANOTHER BIG SUPLEX.

ANGLE WITH AN ANKLE LOCK ON ORTON! HE COULD RETAIN THE TITLE!

MYSTERIO MAKES THE SAVE.

ANGLE WITH ANOTHER AMAZING SUPLEX – THIS ONE OFF THE TOP ROPE!

THE HIGH-FLYING REY MYSTERIO TAKES ANGLE DOWN!

AND HE TAKES DOWN RANDY ORTON, HOOKING HIM FOR THE PIN!

HE DID IT! REY MYSTERIO WON THE WORLD HEAVYWEIGHT CHAMPIONSHIP! UNBELIEVABLE!

HE DID IT FOR EDDIE! CONGRATULATIONS, REY!

DESIGN A CHAMPIONSHIP BELT

When John Cena won the WWE Championship, he created a new belt to match his personality. If you won the WWE Championship, what would your new belt look like? Draw in the space below.

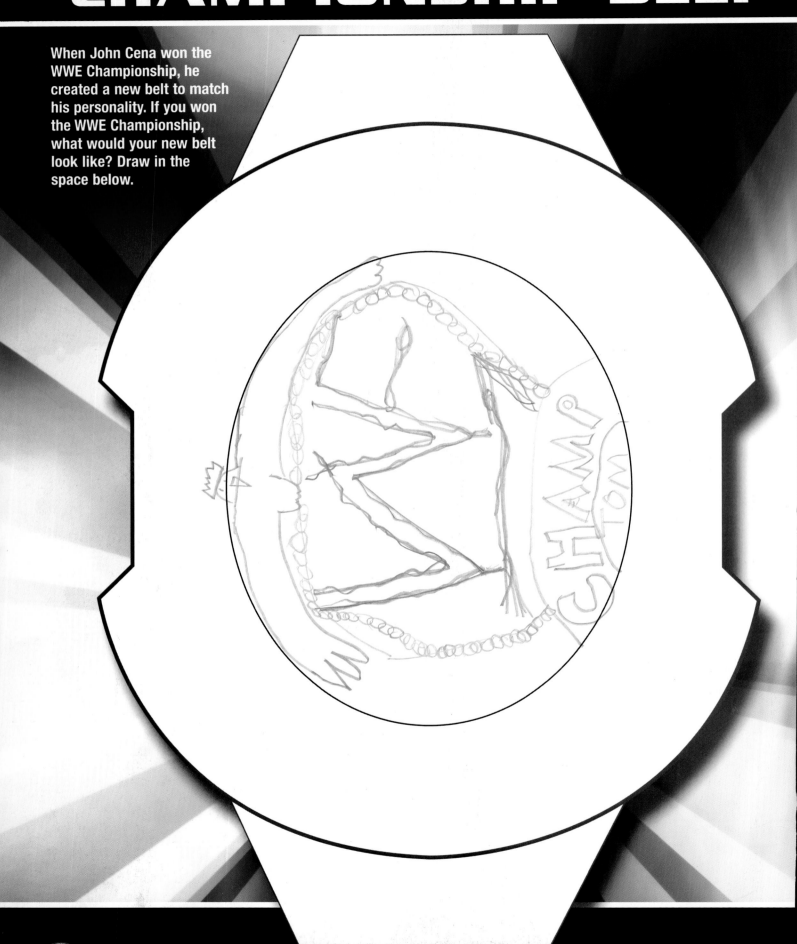

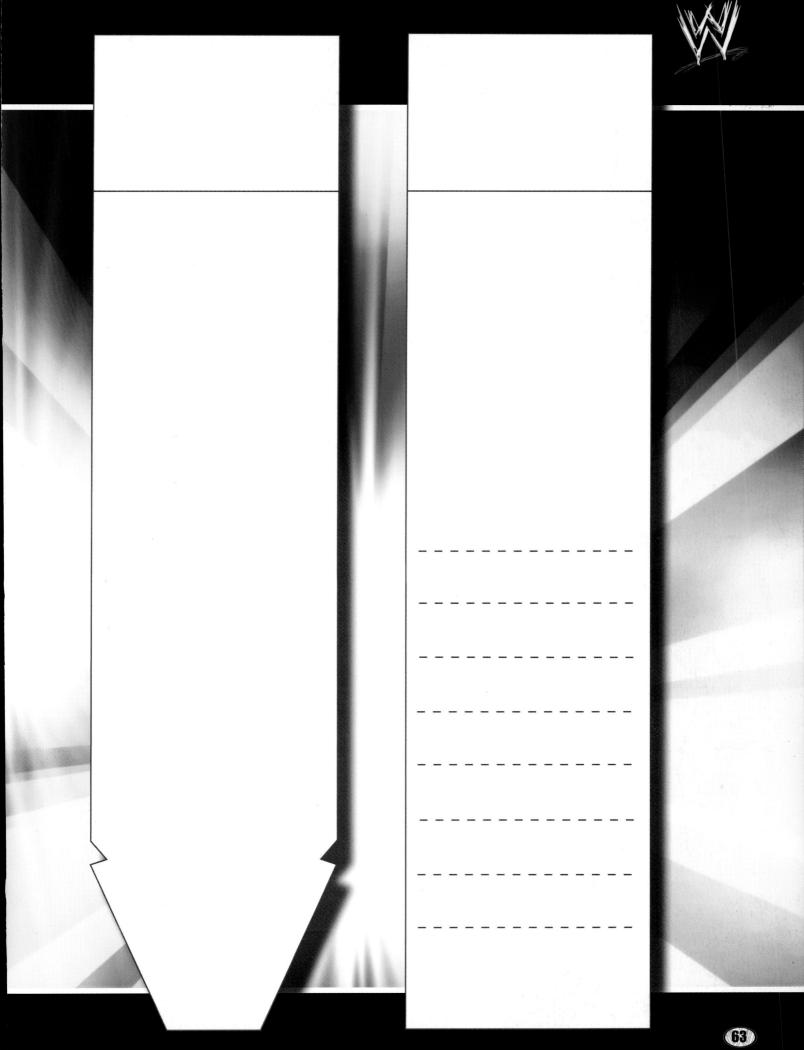

DUSTY RHODES™

Dusty "The American Dream" Rhodes has represented the common man ever since his start in the sport of professional wrestling. With the powerful Bionic Elbow as his finishing maneuver, Dusty beat greats like Harley Race, Terry Funk, and Ric Flair. A multi-time World Heavyweight Champion, this fiery Texan has done it all.

DUSTY LANDS THE BIONIC ELBOW ON TED DIBIASE.

"The Million-Dollar Man"
TED DIBIASE™

His familiar, frightening laugh. His sparkling Million-Dollar Belt. His motto: "Everybody's got a price." "The Million-Dollar Man" Ted DiBiase was known throughout the world. An expert in the ring, DiBiase held the World Tag Team Championship on several occasions, and came close to capturing the WWE Championship using his patented "Million-Dollar Dream" sleeper hold. After retiring from the ring, DiBiase became a manager, working with groups like the nWo, and even Steve Austin!

WITH GREAT MOVES LIKE THIS ONE, TED DIBIASE ALWAYS SHOWED HIS EXPERTISE IN THE RING.

"Mr. Wonderful"
PAUL ORNDORFF™

Don't let his straightforward style fool you. "Mr. Wonderful" Paul Orndorff is a no-nonsense powerhouse in the ring. With his chiseled physique and amazing wrestling skill, Orndorff was a force to be reckoned with in WWE. In fact, he was so powerful that he was one of the participants in the main event at the very first *WrestleMania*. With accolades as both a tag team and singles wrestler, "Mr. Wonderful" is a true WWE legend.

'MR. WONDERFUL' IS IN CONTROL OF YET ANOTHER MATCH.

RODDY PIPER™

This kilt-wearing, bag-pipe playing Superstar has been a part of WWE since nearly the beginning. He's headlined *WrestleMania*, won the Intercontinental Championship, appeared in movies and animated series, worked as the president of both WWE and WCW, and hosted the legendary talk show *Piper's Pit*. Not many people can claim to have made life miserable for Hulk Hogan, but Roddy Piper did just that. You never know when "Hot Rod" might show up, or what to expect when he does. But, can rest assured, that it will be a site to see.

TED DIBIASE IS ABOUT TO FIND OUT WHAT MAKES RODDY PIPER ROWDY!

JUNK YARD DOG™

With his trusty chain always nearby, the late Junkyard Dog was often seen on all fours barking at opponents. He was ready to tear into them like his namesake, and would intimidate and dominate nearly everyone in WWE. Because of this amazing legacy, the Junkyard Dog (or "JYD" as he was also known) was inducted into the WWE Hall of Fame.

JYD IS SURE ENJOYING HIS MATCH AGAINST "MR. WONDERFUL"!

JAKE "The Snake" ROBERTS

Jake "The Snake" Roberts, from Stone Mountain, Georgia, was famous for two things: 1) his devastating finishing move, the DDT; and 2) the large snakes he carried to the ring. Jake "The Snake" was a sinister force, and he knew how to get inside his opponents' heads. And after he soundly defeated them with the DDT, Jake would cover them with one of his trusty snakes. Though he also wrestled for WCW and ECW, it was in WWE that Jake "The Snake" Roberts became a household name.

EARTHQUAKE KNOWS A LOT ABOUT TREMORS, BUT HE'S NEVER FELT SHAKEN LIKE HE WILL AFTER FEELING THE DDT!

SGT. SLAUGHTER™

Attention! The former WWE Champion, Sgt. Slaughter is present! A former U.S. Marine drill instructor, Sgt. Slaughter reined supreme in the '80s and '90s, capturing the WWE Championship from Ultimate Warrior. His patented finishing hold, the Cobra Clutch, led him to victory over many WWE Superstars over the years. After retiring from the ring, Slaughter became the WWE Commissioner, putting him at odds with WWE Superstars Shawn Michaels and Triple H, then known as D-Generation X.

ALWAYS A PROUD AMERICAN, SGT. SLAUGHTER DEFENDED HIS COUNTRY AGAINST THE SOVIET UNION'S NIKOLAI VOLKOFF.

"Superstar"
BILLY GRAHAM™

He was the first true WWE Superstar. So much so, that it was his nickname! "Superstar" Billy Graham was a mountain of a man, with rock-solid muscles and powerful wrestling moves. He could (and did) beat just about anyone. But even more than his in-ring prowess, Graham was known for his flamboyant attire. Tie-dye, feather boas, sunglasses, and more, he was always identifiable. He defeated the great Bruno Sammartino to win the WWE Championship in 1977.

THE 'SUPERSTAR' IS CLOSE TO WINNING ANOTHER ONE!

W eighing in at over 400 pounds, the mighty Earthquake was as big a natural disaster for his opponents as his name implied. His violent "tremors" often resulted in broken ribs for his opponents – including Hulk Hogan, whom the Earthquake put in the hospital for several weeks. He was a World Tag Team Champion with his partner Typhoon as part of the legendary team "The Natural Disasters." Together, they weighed close to half a ton!

IN ADDITION TO HIS POWERFUL TREMORS, EARTHQUAKE COULD BEAT OPPONENTS WITH A VARIETY OF WRESTLING MOVES.

MR. PERFECT™

Not many people can claim to be perfect and then back it up, but the late Mr. Perfect, could! He was a phenomenal technical wrestler, with an ability to go toe-to-toe with the best in WWE history. He held a number of championships in both WWE and WCW, and was a member of the Heenan Family, the nWo, the West Texas Rednecks, and the legendary Four Horsemen. From Minneapolis, Minnesota, Mr. Perfect was a second-generation superstar, the son of Larry "The Axe" Hennig. He was known to occasionally wrestle as his father's tag team partner.

MR. PERFECT IS SHOWING ANOTHER OPPONENT, WHAT IT MEANS TO BE 'ABSOLUTELY PERFECT!'

"The British Bulldog"
DAVEY BOY SMITH™

BRITISH BULLDOG™

He was one-half of the legendary tag team, The British Bulldogs. But after splitting with his long-time tag team partner, the Dynamite Kid, Davey Boy Smith went on to become a legend on his own! Holding the Intercontinental, World Tag Team, and European championships in WWE, as well as titles in WCW, Smith proved himself to be as dominant as he appeared. He married into the legendary Hart wrestling family, becoming a member of The Hart Foundation. At *SummerSlam 1992* in Wembley Stadium, Smith defeated his brother-in-law, Bret "Hit Man" Hart in front of over 80,000 of his countrymen.

FEW COULD MATCH THE STRENGTH OF THE BRITISH BULLDOG. CERTAINLY NOT JAKE 'THE SNAKE' ROBERTS!

DOINK™

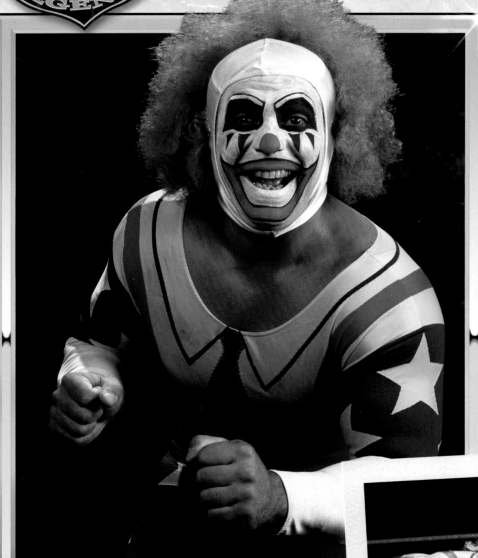

Sometimes he made children laugh; sometimes he made them cry. No one ever really knew if Doink was going to be the "good clown" or the "evil clown" on a particular night, and that made everything harder for his opponents. Even though he looks a little silly, Doink was a strong technical wrestler, beating many of the WWE's top Superstars. He was often accompanied by his small look-alike companion, Dink, or even full-sized doubles of Doink himself! No matter what, matches with Doink were always unusual and unpredictable.

BAM BAM BIGELOW WAS A RUGGED SUPERSTAR. BUT HERE, DOINK REMINDS HIM THAT EVEN THE TOUGHEST MEN COULD BE BEATEN BY A CLOWN.

CARLITO

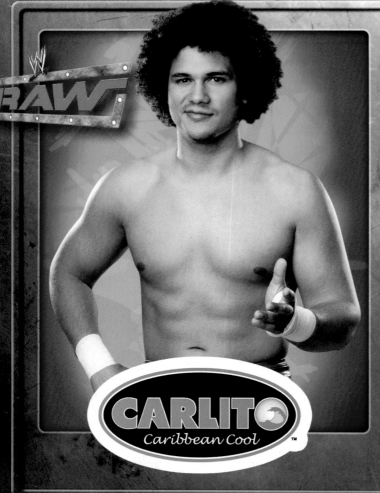

CARLITO
Caribbean Cool

HEIGHT: 5-foot-10
WEIGHT: 234 pounds
FROM: The Caribbean
FINISHING MOVE: Modified Swinging Neckbreaker
CAREER HIGHLIGHTS: Intercontinental Champion, United States Champion

He spits in the face of people who don't want to be cool! Plus he is a talented wrestler, and was the host of his own talk show, *Carlito's Cabana*. After unsuccessfully wrestling for the World Tag Team Championship at *WrestleMania 22*, Carlito turned on his former friend and tag team partner, "The Masterpiece" Chris Masters. Now, that's cool!

SHAWN MICHAELS

HEIGHT: 6-foot-1
WEIGHT: 225 pounds
FROM: San Antonio, Texas
FINISHING MOVE: Sweet Chin Music
CAREER HIGHLIGHTS: WWE Champion, World Heavyweight Champion, *Royal Rumble* Winner, Intercontinental Champion, World Tag Team Champion

"The Heartbreak Kid" Shawn Michaels has done it all. He's held every major WWE championship, and battled the biggest names in WWE history. He even wrestled WWE Chairman Mr. McMahon's son Shane on *Saturday Night's Main Event*, and even the boss himself in a No Holds Barred war. He has to proven that he is the icon of WWE.

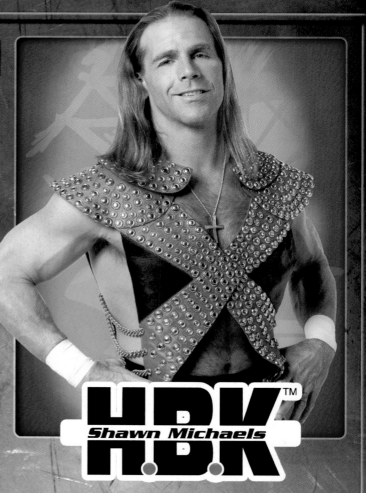

H.B.K
Shawn Michaels

MICK FOLEY™

MICK FOLEY

HEIGHT: 6-foot-2
WEIGHT: 287 pounds
FROM: Long Island, New York
FINISHING MOVE: Mandible Claw
CAREER HIGHLIGHTS: WCW Tag Team Champion, ECW Tag Team Champion

Known for his hard falls, and incredible pain threshold, "The Hardcore Legend" returned to WWE at *WrestleMania 22* to face Edge in a Hardcore Match where they used everything but the kitchen sink against each other. Colourful and generally happy, he hopes you "Have a nice day!"

TRIPLE H®

HEIGHT: 6-foot-4
WEIGHT: 260 pounds
FROM: Greenwich, Connecticut
FINISHING MOVE: The Pedigree
CAREER HIGHLIGHTS: WWE Champion, Intercontinental Champion, World Tag Team Champion, King of the Ring, *Royal Rumble* Winner

Very few can say they've done as much as Triple H. He has defeated the greats in the business, and won more championships than almost any other. At *WrestleMania 22*, the self-proclaimed "King of Kings," wrestled John Cena, hoping to become a World Champion.

TRIPLE H

SMACK DOWN

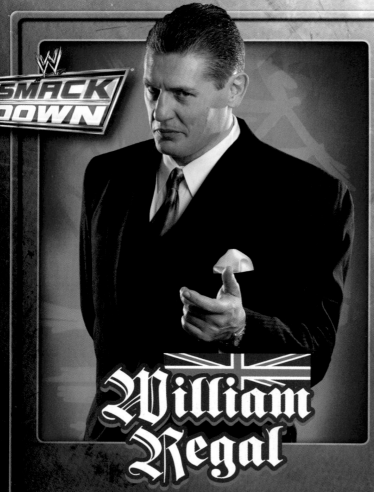

William Regal

WILLIAM REGAL™

HEIGHT: 6-foot-2
WEIGHT: 245 pounds
FROM: Blackpool, England
FINISHING MOVE: The Power of the Punch
CAREER HIGHLIGHTS: WWE Commissioner, WCW Television Champion, Intercontinental Champion, World Tag Team Champion

This rough and tough brawler from the United Kingdom loves the feeling of beating his opponents. Wrestling since he was 15 years old, Regal has experience and knowledge that help him defeat numerous adversaries in WWE. Recently besmirched by Paul Birchill, Regal has sworn revenge against his former protégé.

KEN KENNEDY™

HEIGHT: 6-foot-2
WEIGHT: 243 pounds
FROM: Green Bay, Wisconsin

Most wrestlers pride themselves on their in-ring talents. Mr. Kennedy (as he likes to be known), is most proud of his ring announcer skills. Announcing his own entrance has turned a lot of heads and raised several eyebrows, but in spite of this, Mr. Kennedy has also shown that he has the ability to punish his opponents too.

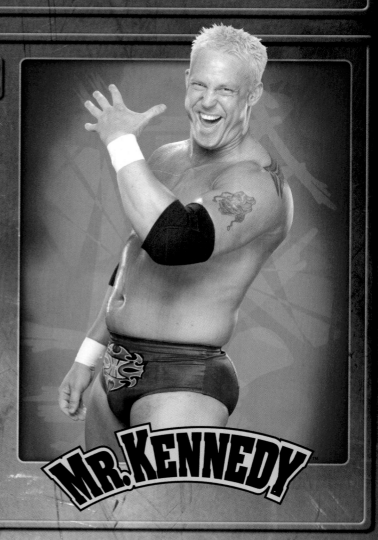

MR. KENNEDY

FINLAY™

HEIGHT: 6-foot-2
WEIGHT: 235 pounds
FROM: Belfast, Ireland
FINISHING MOVE: Emerald Fusion
CAREER HIGHLIGHTS: U.S. Champion, WCW Television Champion

A tough brawler from the mean streets of Belfast, Finlay has been dominant since his return to the ring in 2005. His violent matches with Lashley have been almost too intense for television! And that's how Finlay likes it.

KURT ANGLE®

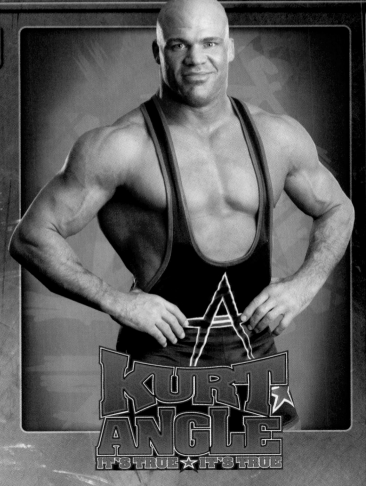

HEIGHT: 6-foot-2
WEIGHT: 220 pounds
FROM: Pittsburgh, Pennsylvania
FINISHING MOVE: Angle Slam, Ankle Lock
CAREER HIGHLIGHTS: World Heavyweight Champion, WWE Champion, WWE Tag Team Champion, Intercontinental Champion, 2000 King of the Ring

A brilliant technical wrestler, the WWE's only gold medal winner has proven time and time again that he is one of the best wrestlers in the world. At *WrestleMania 22* he defended the World Heavyweight Championship against two of the WWE's best. Though he wasn't beaten in the match, he still lost the title. But you can bet Kurt will be back on top of the mountain soon.

THE SPIRIT SQUAD

SPIRIT SQUAD™

MEMBERS: Mikey, Kenny, Johnny, Mitch, Nicky
CAREER HIGHLIGHTS: World Tag Team Champions

The five members of the WWE's own cheerleading team, the Spirit Squad, may look a little goofy, but in actuality they are four tough men. Defeating Kane and Big Show to win the World Tag Team Championship shortly after *WrestleMania 22*, they proved themselves to be as powerful as they are excited!

EUGENE™

HEIGHT: 6-Foot-1
WEIGHT: 238 Pounds
FROM: Louisville, Kentucky
FINISHING MOVE: Rock Bottom, Stunner, Hogan Legdrop
CAREER HIGHLIGHTS: World Tag Team Champion, Winner of Kurt Angle Invitational

The innocent and carefree Eugene grew up being a huge WWE fan. He remembers all the greats, and has modeled his style after the best of the best – even using their moves! He is a hard worker with a special appreciation for WWE history. His future is bright, especially if he keeps imitating the legends.

Eugene™

MATT STRIKER

WEIGHT: 237 Pounds
FROM: New York City, New York
CAREER HIGHLIGHTS: "Teacher" of his own "Classroom" on WWE programming

A former school teacher who was forced to resign in reaction to his wrestling career, Striker is a smart ring technician. Trained by WWE Hall of Famer Johnny Rodz, Striker entered the WWE after wrestling in Japan and elsewhere. With talents both in and out of the ring, Striker has a lot to teach the WWE Superstars and fans.

MATT STRIKER

SNITSKY

WEIGHT: 300 Pounds
FROM: Nesquehoning, Pennsylvania
FINISHING MOVE: Pump-handle Slam
CAREER HIGHLIGHTS: Defeated Kane in Weapon of Choice Match

A monster in the ring, Snitsky was known for attacking Lita and his intense rivelry with Kane. After destroying the "Big Red Monster" in a Weapon of Choice Match, Snitsky entered the tag team ranks, looking to someday win the World Tag Team Championship, and make life miserable for the Raw Superstars.

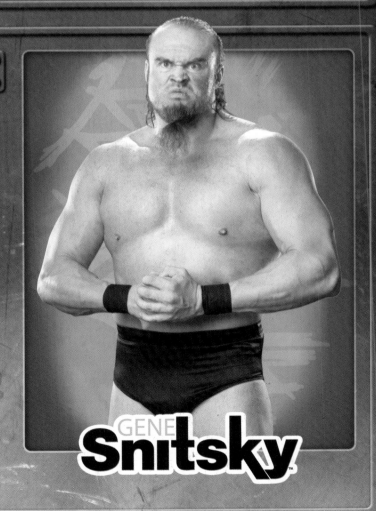

GENE **Snitsky**

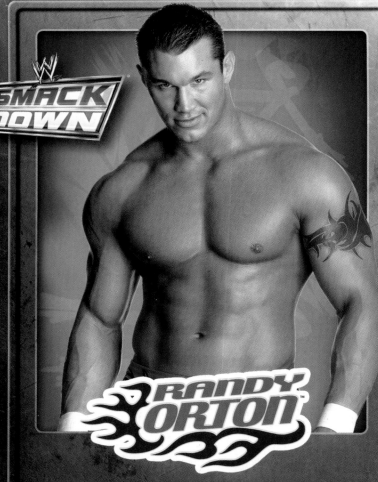

RANDY ORTON™

HEIGHT: 6-foot-4
WEIGHT: 245 pounds
FROM: St. Louis, Missouri
FINISHING MOVE: RKO
CAREER HIGHLIGHTS: World Heavyweight Champion, Intercontinental Champion

A third-generation WWE Superstar, Randy Orton rose to prominence, becoming the youngest World Champion in WWE history. Using his smarts, Randy tricked Rey Mysterio into giving up his shot at the World Heavyweight Championship at *WrestleMania 22*. Randy may have come up short at the big event, but that hasn't stopped him from making Rey's life miserable.

UNDERTAKER®

HEIGHT: 6-foot-10
WEIGHT: 328 pounds
FROM: Death Valley
FINISHING MOVE: Chokeslam, Tombstone, Last Ride
CAREER HIGHLIGHTS: WWE Champion, WWE Tag Team Champion, WCW Tag Team Champion, 14-0 at *WrestleMania*

The man from the dark side is a terrifying force to be reckoned with in WWE. For over 15 years, he has buried countless opponents, and won many championships. His most astounding achievement is an unprecedented 14 - 0 record at *WrestleMania* over the years. Will anyone break his undefeated streak?

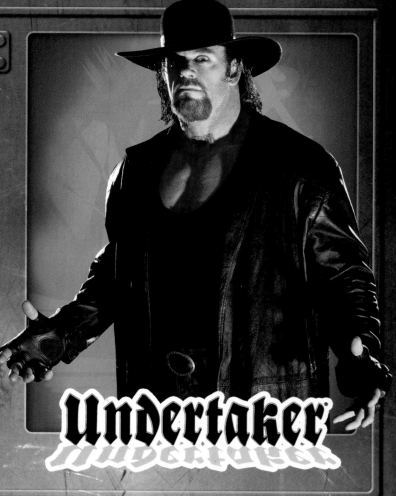

BOOKER T™

HEIGHT: 6-foot-3
WEIGHT: 250 pounds
FROM: Houston, Texas
FINISHING MOVE: Scissor Kick, Book-End
CAREER HIGHLIGHTS: WCW Champion, United States Champion, Tag Team Champion, Intercontinental Champion, WCW Tag Team Champion, WCW Television Champion

With his wife Sharmell nearby at all times, Booker T is a dominant force in WWE. He's held numerous championships. At *WrestleMania 22* he squared off against the mysterious Boogeyman who had haunted Booker and Sharmell for weeks prior to the event.

MARK HENRY™

HEIGHT: 6-foot-1
WEIGHT: 380 pounds
FROM: Silsbee, Texas
FINISHING MOVE: World's Strongest Slam

The World's Strongest Man, Mark Henry, is known as a powerhouse in the ring. An immoveable object, Henry's recent feuds with Undertaker and Kurt Angle have proven to be tough obstacles for the former World Champions. His great strength and athletic ability make Mark Henry one of the toughest Superstars on the WWE roster.

Melina™

From: Los Angeles, California

Career Highlights: Managed MNM to three WWE Tag Team Championships

Since her arrival in WWE in 2005, Melina has led the dominant tag team MNM to the top spot of tag team wrestling. Cameras love her, and she loves them, posing for pictures along the red carpet whenever she gets a chance. She has also wrestled for the Women's Championship. Though she's never won the prestigious title, Melina doesn't care. She's too focused on leading MNM to continued greatness.

Jillian™

From: Los Angeles, California

Jillian is one smart Diva! She has assisted WWE Superstars like MNM and JBL not only in winning matches, but also in their public image. A public relations expert, Jillian will do anything to make her clients look good – including help them cheat to win championships. It's all about image, though, and as long as she's standing with a champion, her image is perfect!

Lilian Garcia™

From: New York, New York

Career Highlights: Monday Night Raw Ring Announcer

Hers is the most identifiable voice in the WWE. Lilian Garcia spends her Monday Nights behind a microphone announcing the WWE Superstars as they compete on *Raw*. She is also an accomplished musician, having released vocal recordings, and singing the American national anthem at several WWE events. She's even been known to get in the ring now and then, facing WWE Superstars.

Ashley™

Height: 5-Foot-5

From: New York, New York

Career Highlights: Winner of the 2005 Raw Diva Search Contest, Multiple Beauty Pageant Winner, Magazine Model, Managed Johnny Nitro to Intercontinental Championship

Ashley was a gymnast, an athlete, a television personality, a model, and a beauty queen all before entering the WWE. With the help of her best friend Trish Stratus, Ashley is growing into a dominant performer in the ring. She's defeated her rivals like Victoria, and promised soon she'll wear the WWE Women's championship.

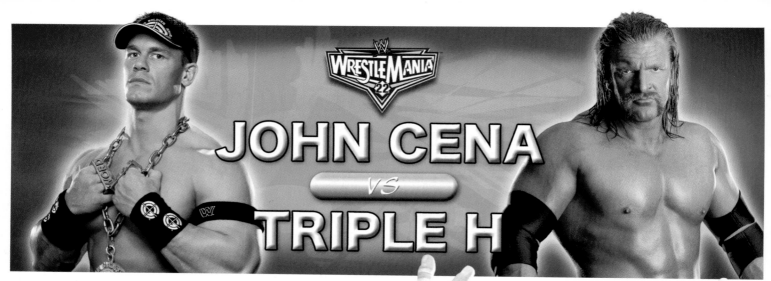

JOHN CENA
VS
TRIPLE H

TRIPLE H, DRESSED AS A KING! HE'S BEEN A WORLD CHAMPION 10 TIMES. YOU KNOW HE WANTS TO MAKE THIS NUMBER 11.

HE'S TOUGH, NO DOUBT ABOUT IT. JOHN CENA WILL HAVE HIS HANDS FULL TONIGHT.

THERE'S A REASON HE CALLS HIMSELF THE KING OF KINGS!

IT'S BECAUSE HE'S BEATEN THE BEST SUPERSTARS IN THE WORLD TODAY!

CENA GETS SOME OFFENSE IN, THROWING TRIPLE H TO THE CORNER.

AND LANDING SOME BIG FISTS.

CENA EVEN GETS IN A HEADLOCK OF HIS OWN.

CENA SENDS TRIPLE H DOWN HARD!

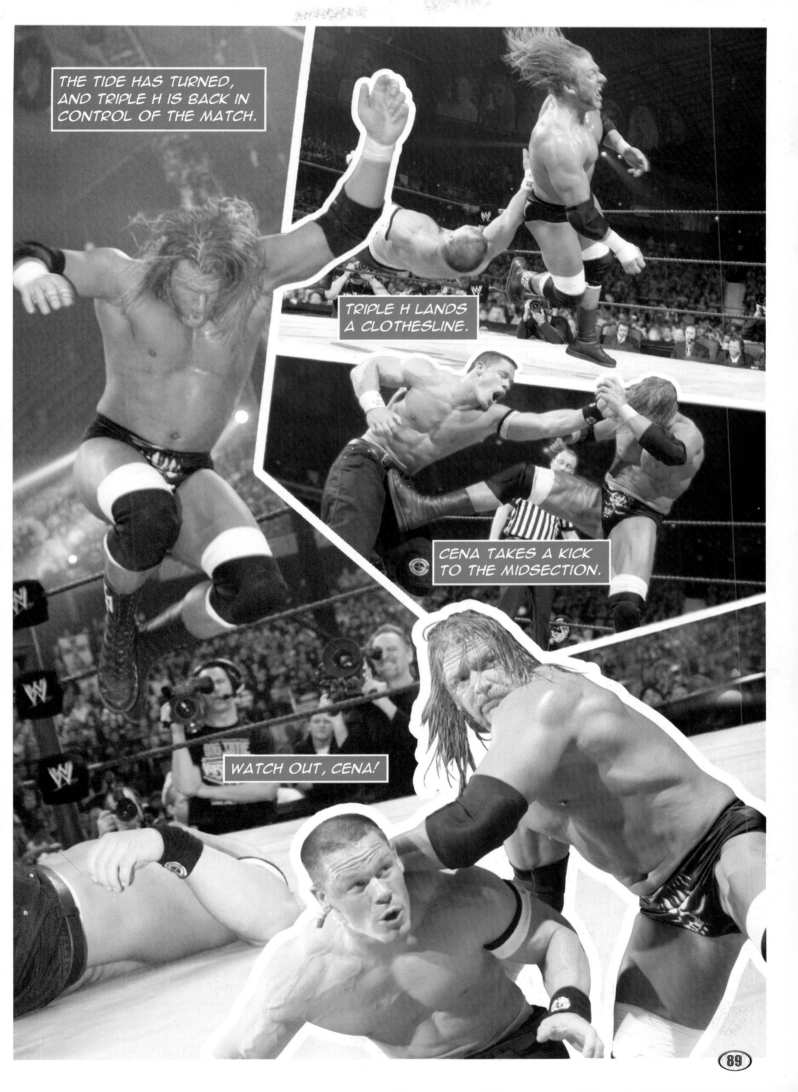

THE TIDE HAS TURNED, AND TRIPLE H IS BACK IN CONTROL OF THE MATCH.

TRIPLE H LANDS A CLOTHESLINE.

CENA TAKES A KICK TO THE MIDSECTION.

WATCH OUT, CENA!

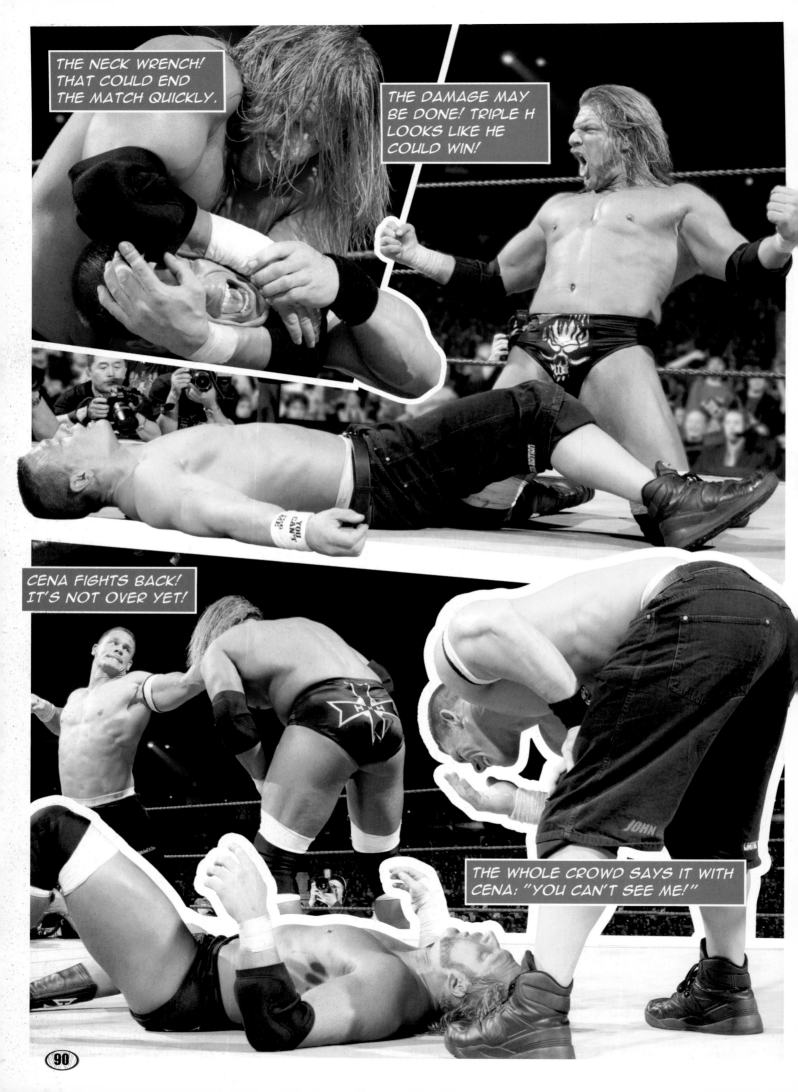

A SHOULDER TACKLE. CENA IS REGAINING THE ADVANTAGE IN THIS MATCH.

WITH A FIVE-KNUCKLE SHUFFLE, CENA COULD PUT "THE GAME" AWAY.

CENA LOCKS IN THE STFU! WILL TRIPLE H GIVE UP?

TRIPLE H IS REACHING FOR THE ROPES. IF HE GETS THERE, CENA WILL HAVE TO BREAK THE HOLD.

HE BROKE THE HOLD, BUT WILL TRY A FU! CAN TRIPLE H ESCAPE?

TRIPLE H ESCAPED FROM THE FU! CENA FLIES FROM THE TOP ROPE.

CENA HAS BEATEN SOME OF THE BEST WWE SUPERSTARS WITH THIS MOVE.

HE COULD DEFEAT TRIPLE H WITH IT, TOO!

WELL, WHADDAYA KNOW?

Do you remember the legends? Superstars like Hulk Hogan, Andre the Giant, and "Rowdy" Roddy Piper paved the way for the Superstars of today. Take the quiz and see if you are worthy of being called Legendary! The answers are at the bottom of the page.

1

Road Warriors Hawk and Animal were better known as what tag team?
A) Demolition
B) Legion of Doom
C) Nasty Boys

2

Which of the following tag teams was never managed by "The Mouth of the South" Jimmy Hart?
A) Orient Express
B) Hart Foundation
C) Hulk Hogan and Brutus Beefcake

3

Where was the Big Boss Man's hometown?
A) Cobb County, Georgia
B) Cell Block D
C) Montreal, Quebec, Canada

4

Who wrestled Shawn Michaels in the infamous main event of *Survivor Series 1997* in Montreal?
A) Diesel
B) Razor Ramon
C) Bret Hart

5

Which of the following was NOT one of the "Natural Disasters?"
A) Earthquake
B) Tsunami
C) Typhoon

6

Who inducted "Mean" Gene Okerlund in the WWE Hall of Fame in 2006?
A) Roddy Piper
B) Hulk Hogan
C) Jimmy Snuka

WWE LEGENDS

7
What 2006 WWE Hall of Fame inductee managed "The Million-Dollar Man" Ted DiBiase?
A) Sensational Sherri
B) Bobby "The Brain" Heenan
C) Jimmy Hart

8
What WWE Legend is The Rock's father?
A) Tony Atlas
B) Rocky Johnson
C) Junkyard Dog

9
Of which team was the late Brian Pillman never a member?
A) Hart Foundation
B) Four Horsemen
C) D-Generation X

10
Who won the WWE Women's Championship at the first *WrestleMania?*
A) Lelani Kai
B) Wendi Richter
C) The Fabulous Moolah

11
What was the name of the live-action television series starring Hulk Hogan?
A) *Mister Muscle Beach*
B) *Thunder in Paradise*
C) *Hulk in Action*

12
In what event did 2006 WWE Hall of Fame Inductee William "Refrigerator" Perry first appear?
A) *WrestleMania 2*
B) *Royal Rumble 1987*
C) *Survivor Series 1997*

Answers: 1.B 2.A 3.A 4.C 5.B 6.B 7.A 8.B 9.C 10.B 11.B 12.A

So, how'd you do?
11-12: Wow! How old are you? You remember everything!
8-10: You could be in the WWE Hall of Fame!
5-7: Back to the gym to build your muscles!
2-4: Good guess, but you're not ready for the ring!
0-1: Time to study the history of WWE.

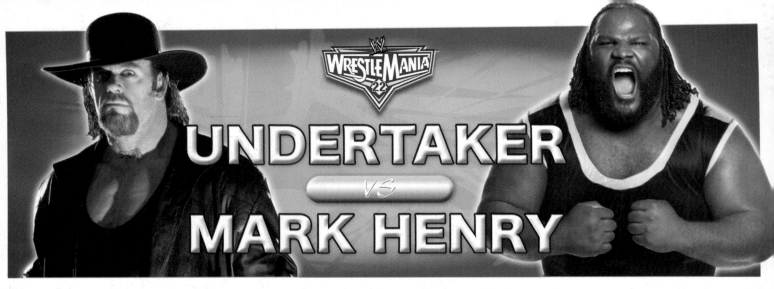

UNDERTAKER
VS
MARK HENRY

THIS IS A UNIQUE MATCH. A CASKET MATCH, WHERE THE ONLY WAY TO WIN IS BY PUTTING YOUR OPPONENT IN A CASKET, AND SHUTTING THE DOOR.

UNDERTAKER'S DRUIDS ARE BRINGING THE CASKET TO THE RING.

MARK HENRY IS THE "WORLD'S STRONGEST MAN", AND COULD PUT AN END TO UNDERTAKER'S 13-0 STREAK AT WRESTLEMANIA.

LOOK AT THE SIZE OF THAT MONSTER! UNDERTAKER SHOULD BE WORRIED.

THE DARKNESS IN THE ARENA IS A LITTLE SCARY.

WHAT IS UNDERTAKER GOING TO DO?

LOOK AT HIS POWERS!

UNDERTAKER INVENTED THE CASKET MATCH, SO YOU HAVE TO BELIEVE THAT HE HAS THE ADVANTAGE.

MARK HENRY DOESN'T WAIT FOR UNDERTAKER. HE OPENS UP THE ATTACK!

THE "WORLD'S STRONGEST MAN" REALLY TAKES IT TO UNDERTAKER.

MARK HENRY WITH THE BIG THROW TO THE ROPES.

IN THE CORNER, MARK HENRY CONTINUES TO POUND AWAY ON UNDERTAKER.

FINALLY, UNDERTAKER GETS A HIT ON HENRY.

BUT MARK HENRY QUICKLY RETAKES THE LEAD.

ON THE OUTSIDE, UNDERTAKER DRIVES HENRY INTO THE STEEL RINGSTEPS.

HE HAS UNDERTAKER RIGHT WHERE HE WANTS HIM.

HENRY GETS HIS REVENGE INSIDE THE RING.

HE IS PUSHING UNDERTAKER CLOSE TO THAT CASKET!

HENRY IS JUST PUNISHING HIS OPPONENT.

UNDERTAKER HAS HENRY IN THE CASKET, BUT HE CAN'T CLOSE THE DOOR!

BOTH MEN ARE IN THE CASKET! WILL ONE OF THEM BE ABLE TO SHUT THE DOOR ON THE OTHER?

IT LOOKS LIKE MARK HENRY MAY HAVE THE ADVANTAGE HERE.

NEITHER MAN WON MATCH. AND NOW THEY ARE BACK IN THE RING.

MARK HENRY HAS BEEN DOMINATING UNDERTAKER THROUGH THIS WHOLE MATCH!

BUT IT LOOKS LIKE IT'S UNDERTAKER'S TURN TO CONTROL THE ACTION.

BUT MARK HENRY TAKES HIM DOWN AGAIN WITH ANOTHER CHOKEHOLD.

AGAIN, MARK HENRY PUMMELS UNDERTAKER.

AND NOW MARK HENRY IS SET UP FOR THE TOMBSTONE PILEDRIVER!

UNDERTAKER TAKES AN AMAZING DIVE TO THE OUTSIDE!

UNDERTAKER GOT HENRY IN THE CASKET AND SHUT THE LID! HE WON THE MATCH!

HE IS STILL UNDEFEATED AT WRESTLEMANIA!

THE "DEADMAN" DEFEATED ANOTHER OPPONENT IN A CASKET MATCH.

THE WINNER ESCORTS THE CASKET TO PARTS UNKNOWN!

WELL, WHADDAYA KNOW?
QUIZ

Think you know the WWE Divas? Take this quiz and see if you know enough to call yourself a ladies man! Answers are below.

1

Who was Trish Stratus's biggest fan?
A) Victoria
B) Mickie James
C) Torrie Wilson

2

What is Torrie Wilson's dog's name?
A) Chloe
B) Jasmine
C) Stella

3

Who was JBL's Assistant?
A) Sharmell
B) Lilian Garcia
C) Jillian Hall

4

Who helped Randy Orton defeat Booker T in a Best of Seven Series?
A) Sharmell
B) Ashley
C) Lita

5

Who won the 2005 Diva Search Contest?
A) Ashley
B) Trish Stratus
C) Candice Michelle

6

Which Diva was a model on the popular American game show *The Price is Right?*
A) Lita
B) Kristal
C) Victoria

7

With what Latino WWE Superstar did Lita make her debut?
A) Rey Mysterio
B) Chavo Guerrero
C) Essa Rios

8

What is the name of Victoria's signature finishing move?
A) The Diva Dive
B) The Widow's Peak
C) Victoria's Victorious

9

Which Diva was called "Too Hot for Network TV" by *SmackDown* General Manager Theodore Long?
A) Candice Michelle
B) Jillian Hall
C) Kristel

10

Which WWE Diva graduated with honors from the University of South Carolina?
A) Jillian Hall
B) Torrie Wilson
C) Lilian Garcia

Answers: 1.B 2.A 3.C 4.A 5.A 6.B 7.C 8.B 9.A 10.C

So, how'd you do?
8-10: You know a lot about the Divas!
6-7: The Divas are impressed!
4-5: Keep trying.
2-3: Not today.
0-1: Sorry, better keep watching.

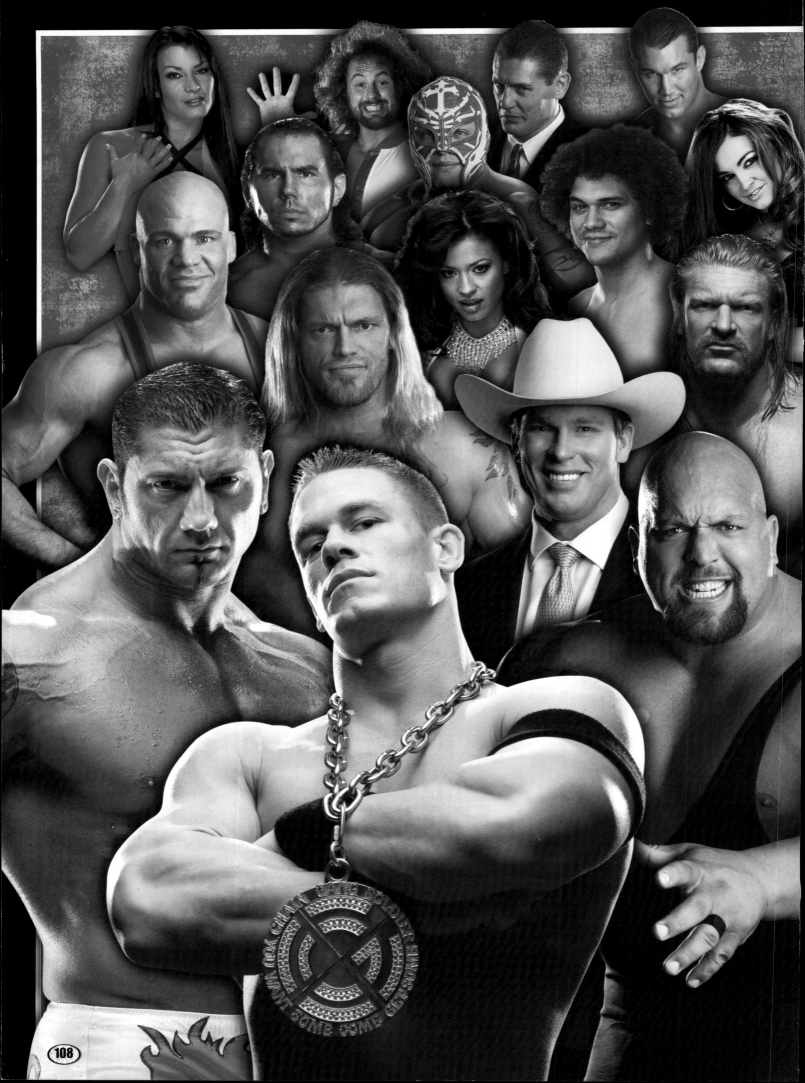

ANSWERS

WORDSEARCH P32

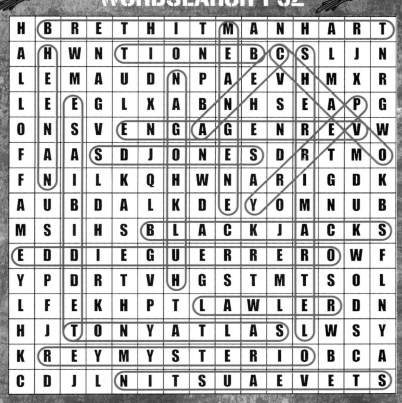

```
H B R E T H I T M A N H A R T
A H W N T I O N E B C S L J N
L E M A U D N P A E V H M X R
L E E G L X A B N H S E A P G
O N S V E N G A G E N R E V W
F A A S D J O N E S D R T M O
F N I L K Q H W N A R I G D K
A U B D A L K D E Y O M N U B
M S I H S B L A C K J A C K S
E D D I E G U E R R E R O W F
Y P D R T V H G S T M T S O L
L F E K H P T L A W L E R D N
H J T O N Y A T L A S L W S Y
K R E Y M Y S T E R I O B C A
C D J L N I T S U A E V E T S
```

CROSSWORD P33

```
R E Y M Y S T E R I O              C
    I                              H
J O H N C E N A         K          R
B   K                   U          I
L   I       R A N D Y O R T O N    S
  E D G E               T          B
    J           B       A          E
R O B V A N D A M   I   N          N
    M           T   G   G          O
    M           R   S   L          I
K A N E   C     R              T
    S H A W N M I C H A E L S
        R       P   O          W
M I C K F O L E Y   L   W
        R       I   E
        I       O
        T R I S H S T R A T U S
        O
        C H R I S M A S T E R S
```